THE LONG TALL journey

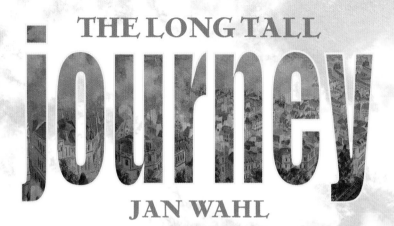

THE LONG TALL journey

JAN WAHL

Illustrated by

LAURENT GAPAILLARD

Designed by Rita Marshall

CREATIVE EDITIONS

Long ago in the land of Sudan
lived a giraffe as tall and elegant as any.
This is her story.

My friends are the monkeys.
We run together,
faster than the clumsy elephant.
But not as fast as the swift wildebeest.

The snapping crocodile is not my friend,
you may be certain.

I eat tender, green leaves from the acacia tree.
I close my eyes to taste them better.

One day, men lead me away from the trees.
I want to cry out, but giraffes have no voice.
Where do they take me?

Goodbye, my monkeys!
Goodbye, egrets!
Goodbye, loud hyenas!
I tremble as I begin the journey.

Storks wheel overhead.
I am given camel's milk to drink—
sweet and warm.

I ride in a boat with red sails down a wide,
blue river. Past strange desert buildings.
Men on the boat stand singing.

We reach a port where three cows,
an antelope, and a noisy parrot join us.

Two young boys attend to me.
Voices call them Hassan and Atir.
They are small, and I kick at them.
The boys speak to me gently
and do not strike back.

•

Now we are at sea. I try to keep
my footing on the pitching deck.
We move farther from home.

Atir feeds me bran and milks the cows.
Hassan gives me shade from the strong sun.
We are in the middle of endless water.

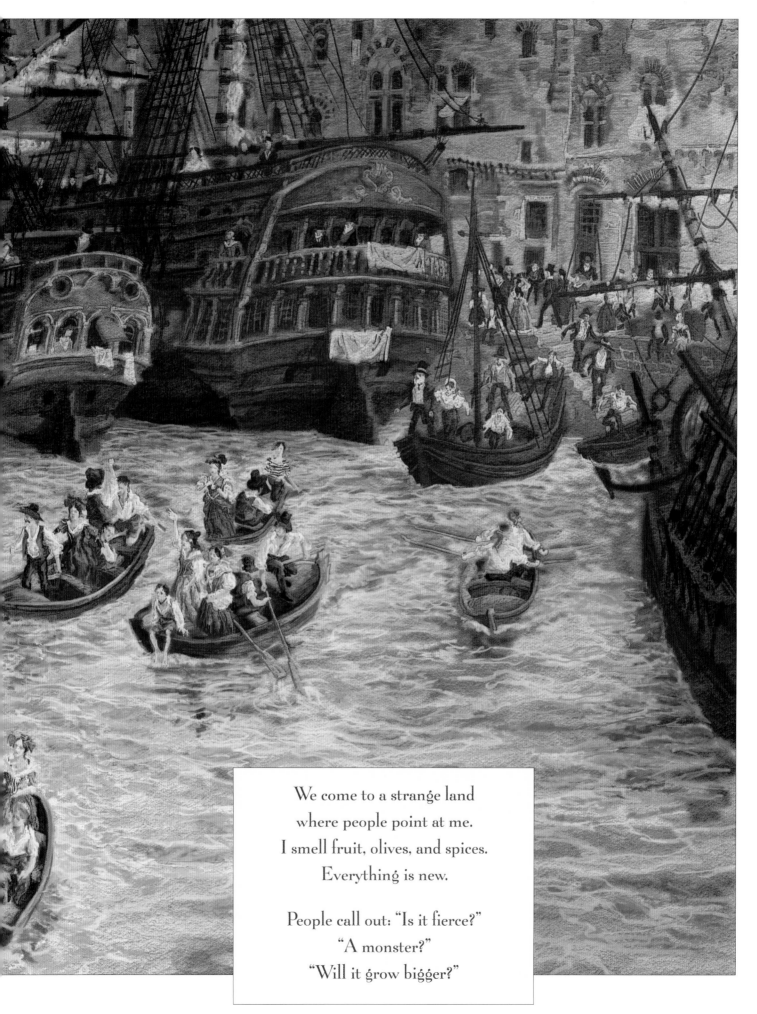

We come to a strange land
where people point at me.
I smell fruit, olives, and spices.
Everything is new.

People call out: "Is it fierce?"
"A monster?"
"Will it grow bigger?"

Next, the boat carries us to a city with
fountains and sweet green grass.

I am led ashore to be met
by a man in a big hat.
Voices call him the mayor.

I am taken across the city to the mayor's house.
The stone road stings my delicate hoofs.
I blink at glowing lamps.

A shed is built to house me and the two boys.
The mayor brings a party of guests
to stare at me.

A woman steps up close.
I pluck a flower from her hair.
Perhaps this is something for my supper?

•

The air soon turns cold.
White flakes fall from the sky.
I shiver and shake.
Hassan covers me with blankets, and
Atir rubs my legs with a warm cloth.

Many days pass. I miss the hot sun.
I miss the sound of monkeys chattering.
I miss the taste of acacia.

At last, the air warms again.
We begin a long, long walk,
passing through a field of sunflowers.

We are six men on horseback,
Atir and Hassan, the milk cows, an antelope,
a wild cat, the parrot, and two wild sheep.

We enter tunnels of trees, walk into rough pine forests, go past orchards with apples and cherries. I eat my first apple.

My feet hurt.
I can walk only a few miles each day.
Where am I going?

In a park,
I graze on a linden tree's leaves.
An old, old woman has been waiting
to pet me.

At sunrise, we enter
the grandest city in the world.
Crowds of people are waiting.

One of the horses bolts.
I follow—dragging the boys behind me.
Men with sticks and helmets
give chase.

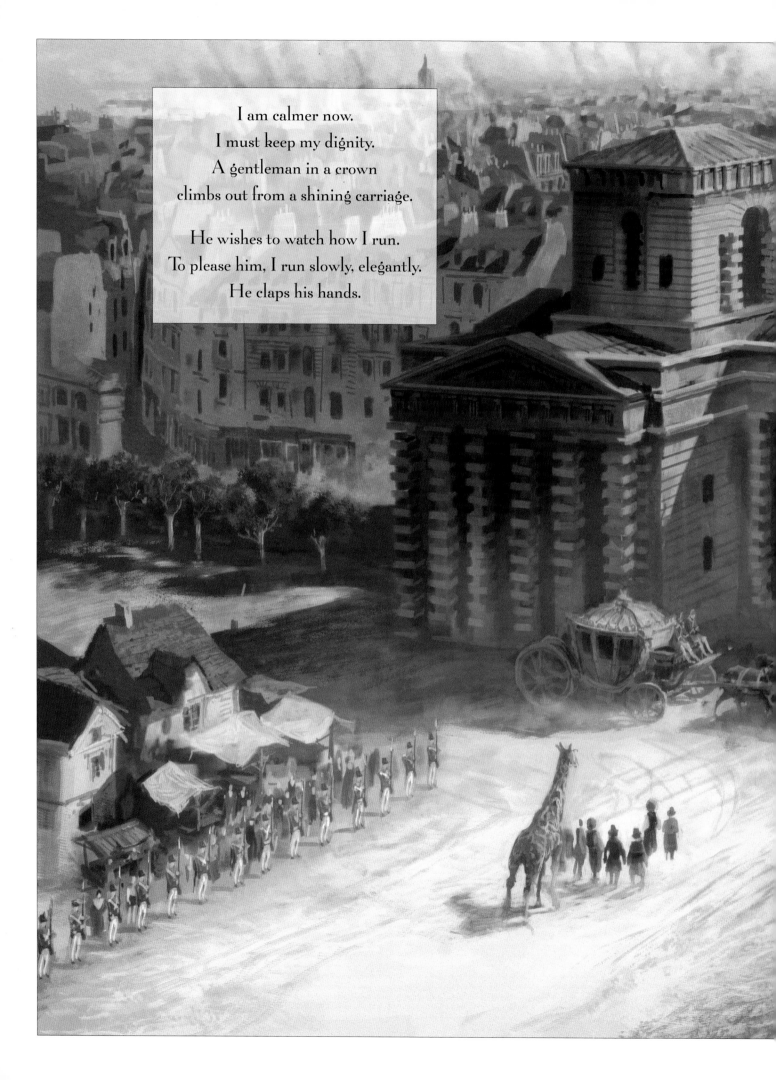

I am calmer now.
I must keep my dignity.
A gentleman in a crown
climbs out from a shining carriage.

He wishes to watch how I run.
To please him, I run slowly, elegantly.
He claps his hands.

Women line the roads,
hair piled high, imitating me.
Children cheer.
Men wear tall hats and flowing ties
with my likeness painted on.

That night, in a splendid garden,
there are fireworks, and music is
played in my honor.

The city stays awake,
and I cannot sleep.

For a time, I live in the garden's house of glass.
Atir has to climb two ladders to scratch
my head. Below, Hassan grooms me.

At last, men build me my own beautiful palace.
It has a fine wood floor and thick,
fresh straw in patterns on the wall.
There are no crocodiles here.

I suppose I will never see my homeland again.
I have traveled too far.

Each night I sleep and dream.
When I awake, I greet my audience.

I nod down to them and see that they are happy.

Then I am happy, too.

Afterword

In 1825, a giraffe, an animal that had not been seen in
the European world for centuries, made the difficult journey
from the highlands of Sudan to the palace of King Charles
X of France. She was a gift from Muhammad Ali, the
Ottoman viceroy of Egypt.

The journey took 2 years and covered 4,000 miles. The
grand parade through France began in Marseille and fin-
ished in Paris—a roughly 500-mile walk requiring 41 days.

The giraffe became a sensation throughout the country.
The animal was pictured on textiles, crockery, soap, knick-
knacks, furniture, and more. A strain of influenza was nick-
named the "giraffe flu," and the newly invented musical
instrument the claviharp was called a "giraffe piano."

France's writers admired the giraffe. As a child, Gustave
Flaubert visited the unique creature. So did Marie-Henri
Beyle (Stendhal). Honoré de Balzac published, in awe, a
love letter to her.

After 18 years of fame in Paris, the giraffe died on January
12, 1845. Nameless in her time, she has since been memorial-
ized as "Zarafa" or known by other terms in ours.

To Eric Honneffer and his mother – J. W. / To all the giraffes who will read this book – L. G.

Text copyright © 2015 by Jan Wahl   Illustrations copyright © 2015 by Laurent Gapaillard   Edited by Kate Riggs   Published in 2015
by Creative Editions   P.O. Box 227, Mankato, MN 56002 USA   Creative Editions is an imprint of The Creative Company
Library of Congress Cataloging-in-Publication Data   Wahl, Jan.   The long tall journey /
by Jan Wahl; illustrated by Laurent Gapaillard.   Summary: In this tale inspired by true events, a giraffe journeys from its home in Africa
to a 19th-century menagerie in France, encountering curiosities and establishing a new purpose in life.   ISBN 978-1-56846-230-1
1. Giraffe—Juvenile fiction. [1. Giraffe—Fiction. 2. Voyages and travels—Fiction.] I. Gapaillard, Laurent, illustrator. II. Title.
PZ10.3.W1295Lo 2015   [E]—dc23   2014038208   First edition 9 8 7 6 5 4 3 2 1